FRESH
ARRANGEMENTS

Mary Gudgeon & John Clowes
M & J PUBLICATIONS

Fresh Arrangements

Mary Gudgeon
& John Clowes

M & J PUBLICATIONS

CONTENTS

First published in Great Britain in 1992 by M & J Publications, The Hollies, Cattlegate Road, Crews Hill, Enfield, Middlesex EN2 9DW. (0992) 461895.

Production Services by Book Production Consultants, Cambridge. Artwork and design by Broxbourne Design (0992) 441726. Printed by Kyodo Printing Co. (Singapore) Pte. Ltd.

ISBN 0 9509748 5 4

Arrangements by Mary Gudgeon and Carol Pritchard (pp. 71 and 79).

OTHER TITLES IN THE SERIES
'Silk Arrangements'
'Christmas Arrangements'
'Dried Arrangements'
'Wedding Bouquets'
See inside back cover for details.

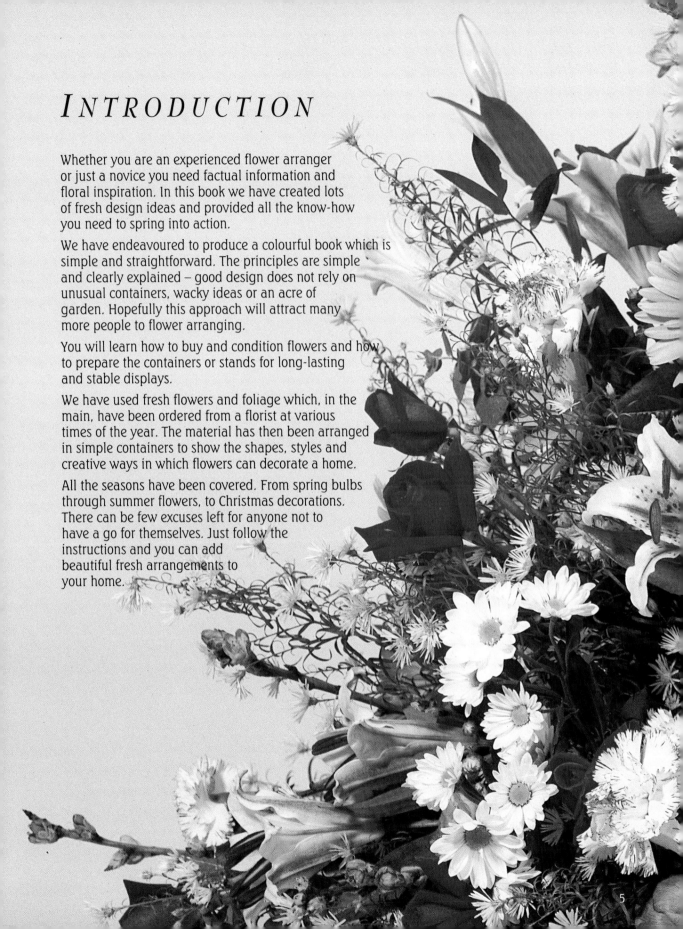

INTRODUCTION

Whether you are an experienced flower arranger or just a novice you need factual information and floral inspiration. In this book we have created lots of fresh design ideas and provided all the know-how you need to spring into action.

We have endeavoured to produce a colourful book which is simple and straightforward. The principles are simple and clearly explained – good design does not rely on unusual containers, wacky ideas or an acre of garden. Hopefully this approach will attract many more people to flower arranging.

You will learn how to buy and condition flowers and how to prepare the containers or stands for long-lasting and stable displays.

We have used fresh flowers and foliage which, in the main, have been ordered from a florist at various times of the year. The material has then been arranged in simple containers to show the shapes, styles and creative ways in which flowers can decorate a home.

All the seasons have been covered. From spring bulbs through summer flowers, to Christmas decorations. There can be few excuses left for anyone not to have a go for themselves. Just follow the instructions and you can add beautiful fresh arrangements to your home.

BUYING FLOWERS

By choice you will use the flowers and foliage that you have grown in your garden or picked from the hedgerow. Nothing will be fresher or last as long. However, very few flower arrangers grow enough material and most have to supplement their stock from a local florist.

The problem then arises of selecting the freshest flowers that are good value for money. If you can choose a ripe melon without the greengrocer throwing you out on your ear you can also use the same senses of touch, sight and smell to judge the best flowers without causing too much upset.

First have in mind the appropriate colours and the amount of material you need to complete the arrangement you have chosen. Your florist may not have in stock the exact flowers you imagined, but suitable alternatives should be available.

Foliage should be bright and fresh. The vase water shouldn't smell stale, and the younger the blooms the better. Watch out for flowers which are not showing any colour at all. For example tulips which are all green may never open. The choice of subject should be young, but not immature.

You should try to buy or pick your flowers at least the day before you wish to arrange them. In this way there will be time for them to be prepared and conditioned for maximum life.

Using flowers in season should be the most economical solution. But remember the world is so small and the demands of the florist industry so great that most flowers can be obtained throughout the year, whatever their origin. Once you build up a relationship with your flower supplier they should be able to obtain most material if you order it in advance.

SEASONAL AVAILABILITY

Flowers are grown for cutting throughout the world. Quick and economic airline transport means that almost all types of blooms are available at major markets throughout the year.

There is no real 'season' for many flowers nowadays. The Flower Council of Holland lists a whole range of blooms that should be available to florists throughout the year. These include rose, carnation, chrysanthemum, Peruvian lily, anemone, anthurium, bouvardia, September flower, delphinium, freesia, gerbera, gypsophila, lily, liatris, sea lavender, Bells of Ireland and trachelium.

With the addition of several types of ferns and foliage, no arranger should be without an adequate choice, whatever the time of year.

What you will notice however is that when flowers are available in quantity then lower prices will result. There are also some flowers and foliage which are rarely made available commercially and you should know when they can be picked from the garden. These are listed below within their season of availability.

SPRING
Apple blossom
Camellia
Catkins
Cherry blossom
Pansy
Solomon's Seal

SUMMER
Buttercup
Columbine
Foxglove
Godetia
Hollyhock
Hosta
Lavender
Lupin
Rosemary
Rue
Whitebeam

AUTUMN
Golden rod
Montbretia
Red hot poker
Rowan berries
Wheat
Zinnia

WINTER
Christmas rose
Dogwood stems
Eleagnus foliage
Holly
Ivy
Pine foliage
Vinca foliage
Witch Hazel

PREPARING THE FLOWERS

Just carrying the flowers home means that they have been out of water for some time. The cut ends will have sealed themselves and when subsequently arranged in a vase or Oasis cannot easily draw up enough water for the flower stem to last its maximum time. All material therefore needs preparation at home to prolong the life of flowers and foliage.

1. CUT AT AN ANGLE

The idea is therefore to re-cut the stem to open up the waterways again. Use a sharp pair of scissors, a knife or secateurs and cut at an angle of about 45 degrees. Take just half an inch (1.5 cm) off at this stage.

Don't smash stems with a hammer. Research shows that this action doesn't help woody stems to absorb water. It is more useful to slit up the length of stem for an inch or so, using sharp scissors or a knife.

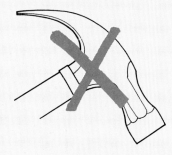

2. STRIP LEAVES AND THORNS

Strip the lower leaves from stems which could decay when under water. Some shrubs such as lilac, veronica, buddleia and viburnum should have all their leaves removed to help prevent the wilting of flowers. At the same time cut off leafy lower branches. Rose thorns can be stripped using scissors to make the stems more easily handled.

3. SOME SHOULD BE HEAT TREATED

Flame Stems which exude sticky material from the cut ends need to be singed with an open flame. Use a candle to seal the ends.

Singe with an open flame: euphorbia, ferns, poppy.

Or Boiling Water Some flowers take up water more readily if the cut stems are given a quick plunge in very hot water. Protect the blooms from steam and dip the ends in boiling water for about 30 seconds. This treatment will also revive flagging rose heads.

Give hot water treatment to: acanthus, angelica, buddleia, celosia, clarkia, cytisus, gerbera, hollyhock, lavatera, magnolia, rudbeckia.

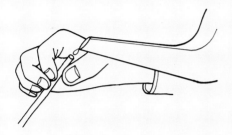

4. FILL UP HOLLOW STEMS

Some stems such as delphinium are hollow and quickly dry out. Before giving them a deep, long drink fill the stems with water and plug the ends with a small piece of cotton wool.

Fill the hollow stems to: delphinium, hippeastrum, hollyhock, lupin.

5. GIVE THEM ALL A LONG DRINK

The tall green vases and buckets favoured by florists are not just for show. They do a useful job in giving cut stems a good deep reservoir for maximum uptake of water. You should do the same. Aim to leave all plant material in deep water for at least two hours, preferably overnight. Tepid water rises to the flower heads much quicker than cold water.

Remember to wash out these containers occasionally with diluted bleach to prevent the build up of algae or bacteria which could reduce the life of your flowers.

Wrap tulip and gerbera stems in newspaper before soaking so that the stems stay straight.

6. WIRING

Some flowers with hollow stems can be wired to keep them straight. Without wiring tulips, for example, turn up to the light. Carefully insert the wire into the stem.

7. TREATING THE WATER

Some people swear by fresh tap water, others add proprietary crystals to extend the life of their arrangements.

These materials, such as Chrysal and Bio Flowerlife work by providing sugar to feed the plant material and algicides to stop the water tubes in the stems from blocking and the water in the vase from smelling.

If you are without these proprietary materials one drop of bleach and a teaspoon of sugar to two pints of water will help to extend the life of the arrangement.

Use the solution to soak your foam material or fill the appropriate vase.

CONDITIONING

Probably the most important thing to learn for the prolonged life of an arrangement is the treatment of your material before arranging.

STANDARD TREATMENT

Cut about half an inch (1cm) from each stem. Cut at an angle. Give them a long drink.

African lily (Agapanthus)
Anemone
Anthurium
Antirrhinum
Astilbe
Baby's breath (Gypsophila)
Belladonna lily (Amaryllis)
Bells of Ireland (Molucella)
Brodiaea (Triteleia)
Carnations (Dianthus)
Columbine (Aquilegia)
Daffodil
Dill
Decorative onion (Agapanthus)
Freesia
Cornflower
Dahlia
Gladiolus
Globe amaranth (Gomphrena)
Globe thistle (Echinops)
Golden rod (Solidago)
Iris
Ixia
Ivy
Larkspur
Liatris
Lily
Montbretia
Orchid
Peony
Peruvian lily (Alstroemeria)
Pinks (Dianthus)
Plantain lily (Hosta)
Lady's mantle (Alchemilla)
Love-in-a-mist (Nigella)

Love-lies-bleeding (Amaranthus)
Nerine
Rose
Sea lavender (Limonium)
Saponaria
September flower
Scabious
Solomon's seal (Polygonatum)
Stocks (Matthiola)
Stonecrop (Sedum)
Sweet peas
Trachelium
Tulip* – Wrap in paper
Yarrow (Achillea)

*Also prick stem with a pin below flower head.

SPLIT STEMS

After cutting at an angle, use scissors to cut up stems for an inch or so. This helps woody stems to absorb water. Place in deep water for several hours.

Beech
Birch
Bridal wreath (Spiraea)
Camellia
Chrysanthemum
Eucalyptus
Garrya
Holly
Lilac
Matricaria
Mexican orange (Choisya)
Mock orange (Philadelphus)
Phlox
Rowan (Sorbus)
Senecio

BOILING WATER TREATMENT

Dip stem ends in boiling water for 30 seconds. Remove and place in deep water for several hours.

Angelica
Bear's breeches (Acanthus)
Bellflower (Campanula)
Bouvardia
Broom (Cytisus)
Butterfly bush (Buddleia)
Christmas rose* (Helleborus)
Cock's comb (Celosia)
Cone flower (Rudbeckia)
Godetia (Clarkia)
Hollyhock
Hydrangea
Lenten rose* (Helleborus)
Mallow (Lavatera)
Magnolia
Mimosa
Shruby veronica (Hebe)
Smoke bush (Cotinus)
Sunflower (Helianthus)
Transvaal daisy (Gerbera)
Veronica
Viburnum
Zinnia

*Also prick stem with a pin below flower head.

FILL HOLLOW STEMS

Fill hollow stems with water and plug with cotton wool. Place in deep water for several hours.

Amaryllis *(Hippeastrum)*
Cow parsley
Delphinium
Dill
Hollyhock *(Althaea)*
Larkspur
Lupin

FLAME SEALED

A candle flame will stop the sticky sap extruding from some stems. After singeing place in deep water for several hours.

Ferns
Poppy
Spurge *(Euphorbia)*

CARE AFTER ARRANGING

Position the arrangement for best effect, but realise that a cool, shady spot will provide the ideal conditions for the longest life. Bright sunshine and hot radiators are not the best companions of cut flowers, nor are cold draughts.

Make sure that the foam is kept wet at all times. With a large arrangement you may have to top up the water daily. Use an indoor watering can with a long spout so that water can be poured gently onto the top of the florist's foam.

Remember that leaves and flower petals can absorb water from their surfaces. A gentle mist of tepid water over the whole arrangement every day will help to maintain a cool, moist atmosphere.

THE EQUIPMENT YOU WILL NEED

You don't need a mountain of equipment to prepare your flowers, but an efficient pair of secateurs and a sharp pair of scissors will pay dividends.

1. Scissors
Any scissors will do as long as they are sharp. Ones with serrated edges seem to cut stems more easily.

2. Secateurs
For woody stems a pair of secateurs may be useful.

3. Knife
Keep a sharp kitchen knife for cutting foam blocks and stripping thorns.

4. Buckets
For that conditioning drink before arranging.

5. Watering can
Choose one with a narrow spout for most control.

USEFUL EXTRAS
6. Fine sprayer
A hand sprayer is invaluable for delivering a gentle mist of plain water over the arrangement.

7. Turntable
A luxury which is worth the investment when you are proficient.

THE MECHANICS YOU WILL FIND USEFUL

Don't be frightened of the term 'mechanics' in flower arranging. It only describes the devices and methods which are used to hold flower and foliage stems in position. Here are some of the items you will find useful. On the following two pages you will see how they are used to give you a firm foundation for your flowers.

8. Green florist's foam
Sold under many brand names including 'Oasis', this florist's foam is a vital basis of many arrangements. When thoroughly soaked it provides water and holds stems in exactly the same position as when first pushed into the material. It can be obtained in various shapes and all can be cut with a knife to fit most containers.

9. Foam anchors
This four-pronged anchor, sometimes called a frog, is used to hold foam firmly in the container. The anchor is stuck to the base of the container with Oasis Fix.

10. Oasis Fix
A fixative material also known as adhesive clay used to secure the foam anchor to the base of the container of your choice. 'Oasis Fix' is a brand name for one of these fixatives, but others are just as suitable.

11. Adhesive tape
Useful for taping down blocks of foam. Available in white and green.

12. Chicken wire
Useful for larger arrangements where blocks of foam need extra support. Chicken wire which is coated with green plastic is best.

13. Pinholders
Heavy metal bases which are covered in sharp pins. Flower stems are pushed straight down onto the pins. Well pinholders retain a pool of water, although this will need topping up regularly.

14. Cones and tubes
Used in larger arrangements when fresh plant material needs to be raised above the basic level of the container. If the stem is not long enough, tape the cone or tube to a stick and then push into the foam.

PREPARING THE BASES AND CONTAINERS

THE STANDARD METHOD

1. Find a suitable container or base for the size and shape of the arrangement you have in mind.

2. Push a piece of Oasis Fix or other florist clay onto the flat base of the anchor and push down firmly onto the floor of the container. Use more than one anchor for large blocks of foam.

3. Push the wet foam block onto the anchor.

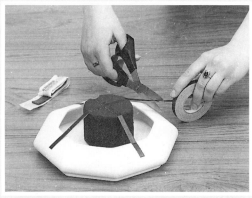

4. Use adhesive tape from one side of the container, over the top of the foam, and stick to the other side of the container. A cross of tape will ensure the foam is held firm.

VARIATIONS

Vase
Place a pin holder into the bottom of the vase. Alternatively push some chicken wire into the mouth of the vase to support the stems.

Wicker basket
Line wicker baskets and anything porous. Either use a polythene bag or a plastic tray as the waterproof base.

Terracotta container
Unglazed clay will absorb water continuously and eventually soak the surface it is standing on. To prevent this, line the terracotta container with polythene. Alternatively you could use a plastic tray which will sit in the neck of the container. Tape this in position for stability.

THE PEDESTAL METHOD

Find a waterproof container which will hold two blocks of Oasis and sits comfortably on the pedestal base.

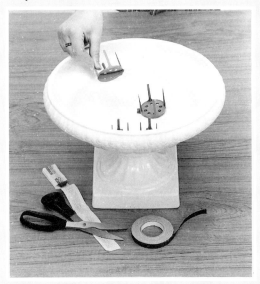

1. Fix four anchors into the base of the container using Oasis Fix or other florist's clay.

2. Take one foam block previously soaked in water and push this onto the anchors at the back of the container in a vertical position. Cut the next block slightly shorter and position this at the front.

3. Use florist tape from one side of the container, over the top of the foam, and stick it to the other side of the container. A cross of tape will ensure the foam is held firm.

4. Use chicken wire or other mesh to go over the foam. Wire into position under the rim.

MAKING BOWS

These bows are made from linen, cotton or polyester material and painted. Worn out men's shirts are ideal as a source of fine cloth.

Each bow is made from two 'tubes' of different sizes.

For the bow cut an oblong 12" (30 cm) by 11" (28 cm). Turn back the edges along the shorter sides and tack a line of stitches along each edge (Fig. 1).

Fold the material in half lengthways and run a line of stitches along this edge (Fig. 2). Turn inside out and you will have a tube of material without any tatty edges.

For the 'tails' of the bow make a similar tube using a piece of cotton approximately 14" (35 cm) by 7" (18 cm).

The tie in the middle is also a piece of the same material approximately 7" (18 cm) by 2" (5 cm). Because the cut edges are not seen it is not necessary to make this into a tube.

Now assemble the three pieces of material to make a bow shape. Keeping the seams to the back, use the tie to attach the tail tube to the bottom of the bow (Fig. 3).

The beauty of these hand-made bows is that they have a three dimensional look and can be made to any size. They are so much more luxurious than ribbon bows. The principle of using stiffened material can also be used to produce decoration for plaques and round wreaths.

To stiffen the material take some universal PVA adhesive (available from any good hardware or DIY shop) and dissolve in the ratio of one part adhesive to 20 parts of water. Stir until the solution is like a thin cream.

Dip the bow into this solution and then squeeze out any excess. Place the bow onto a piece of polythene and start to pull the material into shape. This is the time when you make the tubes of material three dimensional and add the folds and scrunches which are their unique beauty. It will take time, but persevere.

Leave to dry overnight and then paint as required. For Christmas, spray cans of gold paint are ideal. But remember that they can be painted with any colour of emulsion paint to harmonise with a party garland or buffet table.

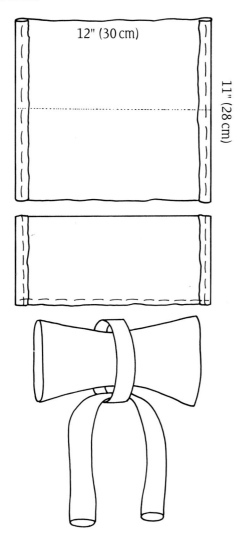

12" (30 cm)

11" (28 cm)

CANDLESTICKS

Creating a flower arrangement on the top of a candlestick is popular. Buy a special candle cup in a colour to match the base and fit into the candlestick using Oasis Fix.

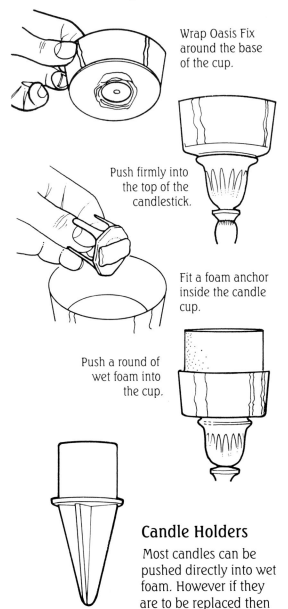

Wrap Oasis Fix around the base of the cup.

Push firmly into the top of the candlestick.

Fit a foam anchor inside the candle cup.

Push a round of wet foam into the cup.

Candle Holders

Most candles can be pushed directly into wet foam. However if they are to be replaced then candle holders are useful. Small plastic holders are available for a few pence which hold a candle firmly and push easily into foam.

WIRING CONES

Wrap a stub wire around the base of the cone so that the wire disappears between the seed husks.

Bend down the two wires until they are side-by-side.

Twist one wire firmly around the other to make a stem.

THE SHAPES TO FOLLOW

Most of the traditional arrangements which are shown in this book follow one or other of the 'basic shapes' which flower arrangers find so useful.

If you can keep your material within one of the outlines shown here you should end up with good proportions, line and balance.

All arrangements should have a height which balances its width and you should choose plant material which falls easily into the shape you have chosen.

If you are a beginner the 'Symmetrical Triangle' or the 'Circular All-Round' shapes are the easiest to master. After you feel more confident, the curved outlines are well worth attempting.

These suggested shapes are presented to help, but not to restrict your own creativity. Modern arrangements are much less formal nowadays and almost any grouping of flowers can be classed as an 'arrangement'. If you achieve a shape which is pleasing, but doesn't fall within these guidelines so well and good.

Remember that the purpose of your arrangement is to display your flowers to the best advantage. If it pleases you and your family that is sufficient – beauty is in the eye of the beholder.

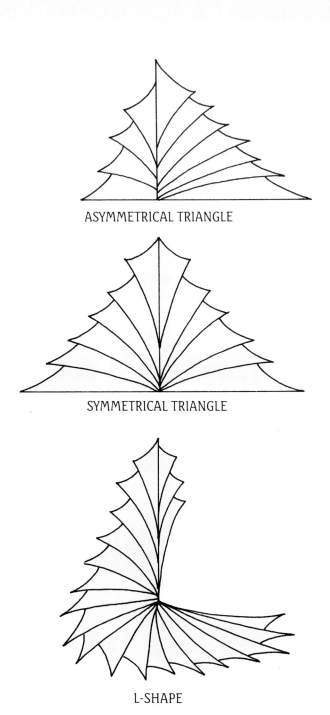

ASYMMETRICAL TRIANGLE

SYMMETRICAL TRIANGLE

L-SHAPE

HORIZONTAL

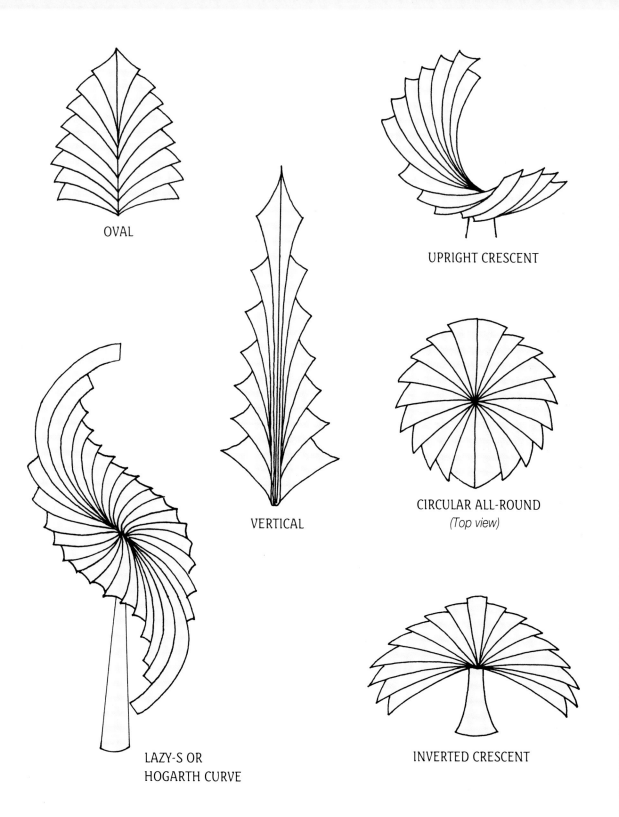

OVAL

UPRIGHT CRESCENT

VERTICAL

CIRCULAR ALL-ROUND
(Top view)

LAZY-S OR
HOGARTH CURVE

INVERTED CRESCENT

FRAGRANT VASE

This classical round design uses sprays of chrysanthemum together with the perfumed heads of bouvardia as the white highlights. The flat flowers are contrasted well using spikes of mauve veronica to break the circular shape.

How it is made

Fix a foam anchor to the base of a plastic saucer. Push on a round of wet foam, previously soaked for a couple of hours. Tape this firmly to the top of the vase using adhesive tape (Fig. 1).

Start by defining the top of the round shape with one stem of bouvardia and two sprays of chrysanthemum. Then make four more radial points with two sprays of chrysanthemums and the trailing ivy at the base (Fig. 2).

Use several spikes of veronica around the edge of the arrangement. Cut the stems accurately so that the base of the mauve flower spike is level with the outer edge of the circle previously defined (Fig. 3).

Fill in the centre with bouvardia and chrysanthemums placed in position with each flower head pointing in different directions. A spike or two of veronica should be positioned in the face of the arrangement to create a feeling of depth.

Fill in the back of the arrangement with any material which is over so that the foam and other mechanics are completely hidden.

The material you will need

12 Sprays of pink chrysanthemum
10 Spikes of veronica *(Veronica exaltata)*
12 Heads of bouvardia
 2 Pieces of variegated ivy

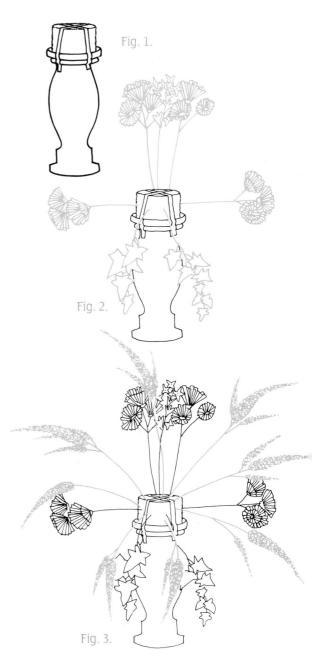

Fig. 1.

Fig. 2.

Fig. 3.

21

CAMELLIA CURVES

The sophisticated blooms of the camellia are usually few and far between so they need to dominate any arrangement. Here their rounded lushness is contrasted with the sharp edges of red flax leaves and a few pink buds of viburnum.

How it is made

Prepare the container in the usual way with two anchors in the base and a block of wet foam pushed firmly home.

Start with the flax leaves to make the top and left points (Fig. 1). The curved shape is made by bending the leaf tip back to the base and stitching wire through the two layers to hold it in shape (Fig. 2).

Position some stems of viburnum and the variegated laurel leaves around the edge of the containers to form the base line of the arrangement. Use a branch of camellia buds near the top and then fill in with the camellia blooms (Fig. 3). Make sure they face in different directions away from the centre.

Position two flax leaves wired into curves in the centre and use viburnum to fill in any obvious gaps.

The material you will need
5 Camellias
8 Decorative flax leaves *(Phormium)*
3 Variegated laurel leaves
5 Heads of viburnum

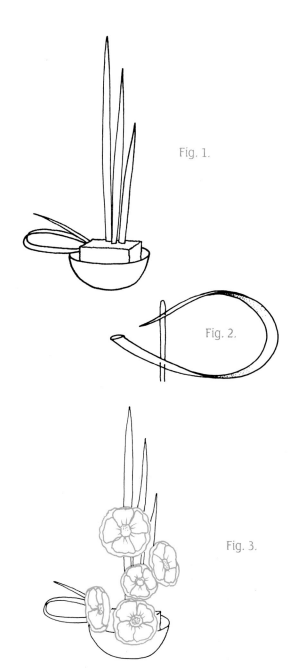

Fig. 1.

Fig. 2.

Fig. 3.

MAUVE TRIANGLE

This large, triangular display uses a wealth of summer flowers to create a beautiful shape filled with a harmonious blend of colours. The outline and scale are the most important aspects of success with these massed arrangements.

How it is made

Fix four anchors into the base of the chosen container which should preferably have a flat bottom so that the wet foam sits square and stable. Soak the wet foam and push onto the anchors. To ensure the foam is held firmly, tape over the top of each block and fix to the sides of the bowl (Fig. 1). Cover with chicken wire.

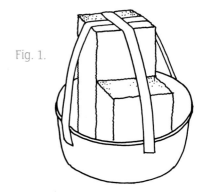

Fig. 1.

Start by defining the points of the triangle shape. In this arrangement the top points are made with pink larkspur and the base points with sprays of chrysanthemums (Fig. 2).

Now define the outline of the triangle using different colours and flowers to give interest.

Work inwards towards the centre, mixing colours and varieties. Always ensure that the stems are seen to be radiating from a central point and recess material deep within the arrangement occasionally to avoid seeing too many stems.

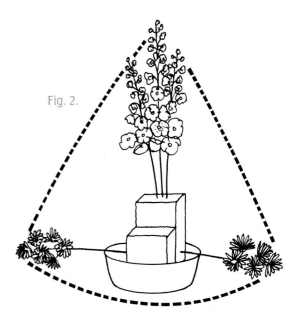

Fig. 2.

Make sure the base line is varied and that there is a focal point in the centre. In this arrangement, one of the five deep mauve stocks, surrounded by white larkspur does this job.

The material you will need
  8 Sprays of pink chrysanthemums
  5 Mauve stocks
16 White larkspur
16 Pink larkspur
12 Peruvian lily *(Alstroemeria)*
  8 Sprays of aster or michaelmas daisy

SALMON SPLENDOUR

This design is a miniature pedestal, showing that the inverted crescent shape works well on a small wrought iron base.

How it is made

Fix a foam anchor into the top metal container with florist's clay. Push on a round of wet foam, previously soaked in water, firmly onto the anchor (Fig. 1).

Start by defining the three major points of the arrangement with roses (Fig. 2). Then take six more rose stems to start the outline (Fig. 3).

At this stage it is a good idea to use the sea lavender to cover the foam and to give a dense feel to the centre.

Use a mixture of carnations and roses to fill in the centre of the arrangement. The flower stems should all seem to radiate from a central point. This will mean that the flowers below the level of the foam will be pointing at the cill.

Some of the flowers should be recessed slightly deeper than others to provide depth. When all the blooms are in position fill any gaps with the sea lavender.

The material you will need
17 Salmon pink roses
13 Pink carnations
10 White sea lavender *(Statice)*

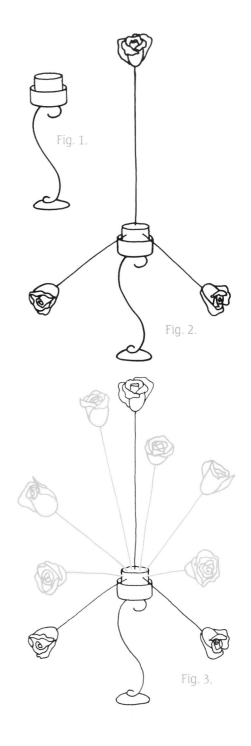

Fig. 1.

Fig. 2.

Fig. 3.

RIOTOUS BASKET

The wide variety of material in this attractive basket bring the vibrance and colour of a garden into the home. A well defined shape holds the informal mixture of flowers together.

How it is made

Find a waterproof container to fit inside the basket and prepare in the standard way. Fix two foam anchors to the base of the container with Oasis Fix. Then push a block of wet foam, previously soaked in water, onto the anchors. If the level of the foam is not above the rim of the basket add another block of wet foam holding it in position with wire grips (Fig. 1). Place the container into the basket and tape into place.

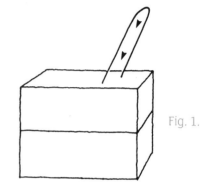

Fig. 1.

Start by creating the three dimensional triangle with delphiniums (Fig. 2). Fill in this outline with other material including some of the astilbe, bright yellow rudbeckia and the purple trachelium.

Ensure the base line is complete using the pink sprays of saponaria and then start to fill towards the centre. Mix the colours and textures of the material ensuring the stems radiate from a central point. Push some material close to the foam to give recessed depth to the arrangement while keeping the echinops above the normal level of the other flowers.

Keep two or three of the bright yellow rudbeckias for the centre to act as the focal point.

The material you will need
10 Cone flower (Rudbeckia)
 5 Bells of Ireland
10 Purple trachelium
10 Pink delphinium
10 Blue delphinium
10 Larkspur
 7 White astilbe
 3 Pink astilbe
 7 Echinops
 5 Saponaria

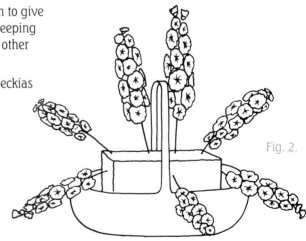

Fig. 2.

PINK & BLUE DELFT

Simple shapes can be just as interesting as complex designs when the material is varied in texture and contrasting in colour. This white bowl is filled with summer flowers of similar scale – a lesson in controlled elegance.

How it is made

The best way to achieve the overflowing base line of flowers shown in this arrangement is once again to use Oasis foam. This allows blooms on straight stems to overhang the edge of the container.

Fit an anchor into the bottom of the container with Oasis Fix. Trim a block of green Oasis to size so that it fits into the vase with at least an inch of the foam appearing above the edge.

Start by going around the edge of the container with an even mixture of carnations, roses and cornflowers (Fig. 1).

Now place the central stem of carnation buds at the right height in the middle. Cut the stems of white matricaria sprays quite short so the flowers are recessed below the dome shaped outline (Fig. 2). This will give depth to the design and cover the foam.

Work around and upwards to gradually fill the dome shape with an interesting mixture of flowers. The sprays of carnations will need to be cut into smaller pieces.

The fern like foliage which is an integral part of love-in-a-mist is vital to add a different texture to the design. Ensure some of these stems are used to break any hard look to the edge of the arrangement.

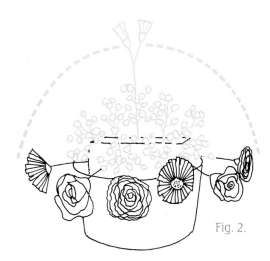

Fig. 1.

Fig. 2.

The material you will need
16 Blue cornflowers
12 Pink roses
 5 Sprays pink carnations
16 Love-in-a-mist *(Nigella)*
 5 Sprays of matricaria

ROSES & BLOSSOMS

This long, low arrangement in red and cream flush is suitable for any display area or can be used as an attractive table centre. While you wait for the buds of the flowering prunus to open the attractive bronze foliage complements the overall colour scheme.

How it is made

Prepare a tray with two anchors fixed to the base with Oasis Fix. Push a block of wet foam, previously soaked for at least 2 hours, onto the anchors. As this is not a tall arrangement no taping is necessary.

Start the arrangement by filling in all round the base with the flowering prunus. Maintain a long shape by keeping the pieces at the side short (Fig. 1).

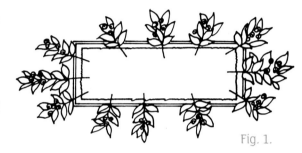

Fig. 1.

Place twelve carnations around the edge, varying the height from the base and the depth into the arrangement of adjacent flowers (Fig. 2). Try to set space between each flower.

Now position the roses, creating an easy dome shape (Fig. 3). If there are any obvious spaces around the bottom fill in with prunus foliage.

Fig. 2.

Place the top-most carnation at a suitable height and then complete the arrangement with more carnations.

The material you will need
24 Carnations
9 Red roses
20 Flowering stems of ornamental
plum or cherry *(Prunus)*

Fig. 3.

BASKET OF SNAPDRAGONS

Only snapdragons (Antirrhinums) bought from a florist could look this good. This is one case when buying beats home grown by a mile. They are used with other material to create a beautiful basket, overflowing with colour and texture. The use of pastel shades will help to create a lightness that complements the attractive basket.

How it is made

A dish, tray or other container is vital to sit inside this low basket or subsequent watering of the foam will be messy.

Prepare the container with two anchors and a large block of wet foam, thoroughly soaked. Tape the block to the tray and to the basket (Fig. 1).

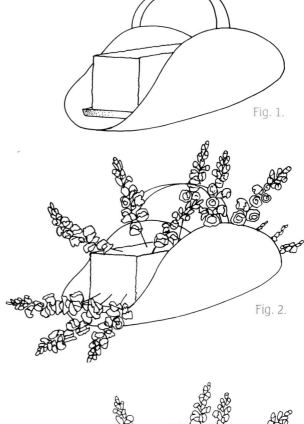

Fig. 1.

Start by using the stems of viburnum to edge the basket. Use pink snapdragons around the edge to continue the flowing lines of the basket. Initially there are three at each end and three either side (Fig. 2).

Build up the flower base using white snapdragons and Peruvian lilies. At each end use the deep coloured spray of chrysanthemums to give a contrast in texture to the spikes of snapdragons (Fig. 3).

Fill the basket with flowers, ensuring some of the viburnum is recessed so that the tray and foam are hidden. The overall effect should be light and summery.

Fig. 2.

The material you will need
16 Pink snapdragons (Antirrhinum)
16 White snapdragons (Antirrhinum)
12 Peruvian lily (Alstroemeria)
 7 Stems of flowering viburnum
 2 Sprays bronze chrysanthemum
 2 Sprays of white chrysanthemum

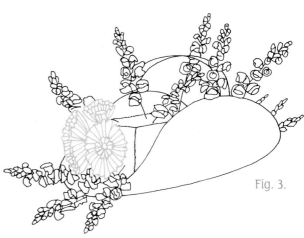

Fig. 3.

SPRING GARDEN

Spring flowers look most attractive when seen to be growing in a miniature garden. In this design we have used moss to give a natural surface for the stems to grow through and to allow the use of a growing plant to be positioned alongside cut flowers.

How it is made

Take a deep ceramic bowl which is big enough to take the roots of a drumstick primula. If the root ball is too deep squeeze the soil gently so that the surface will be below the moss. On one side of the bowl fix two plastic anchors to the base with Oasis Fix. Push a block of well soaked foam onto the anchors.

Knock the drumstick primula out of its pot and position to the right of the foam block (Fig. 1). Pack round with moss to keep the plant in position and to create a level surface all over the bowl.

Now start to arrange the cut flowers, starting with the liatris at the back of the bowl. See that stems come from a common point and ensure that the stems are of different lengths to maximise the beauty of these flowers (Fig. 2).

Select daffodils at different stages of opening and cut to various lengths. Position at the front of the arrangement. To avoid bending the stems you may like to push a pencil into the foam before pushing home the flower stem firmly.

Lastly take a few of the daffodil leaves and use to break up any areas around the base which show too many stems.

The material you will need
    9 Stems gayfeather *(Liatris)*
   11 Daffodils
    1 Drumstick primula plant *(Primula denticulata)*

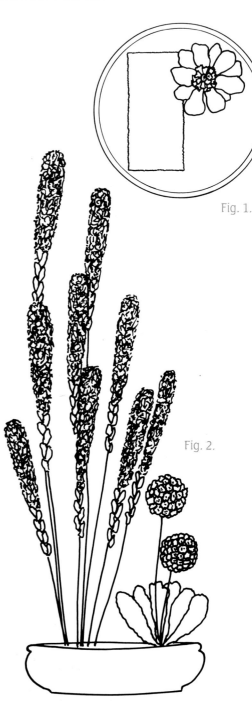

Fig. 1.

Fig. 2.

APRICOT FIREMANTLE

Roses and carnations are an ideal mixture for any arranger. The end result is luxurious and sophisticated enough for any occasion. Perhaps more importantly the cut flowers can be obtained from florists at any time of the year.

How it is made

No special container is necessary. Take a plastic tray and prepare the wet foam as shown on page 14.

As with all triangular arrangements start by defining the three main points (Fig. 1). The carnations as the biggest flowers have been used in this arrangement to further outline the sloping sides of the triangle and to first indicate the depth of the display (Fig. 2).

Before filling in the centre of the arrangement see that some of the baby's breath is used to cover the foam which may later be visible.

The placement of two types of flowers is one of judgement. Avoid a uniform display in straight lines with every flower alternating. This may be the precise way to do it but it can look boring. Instead try to place each flower in its own space. Work from the outside towards the centre, filling in between the stems with white baby's breath as you go.

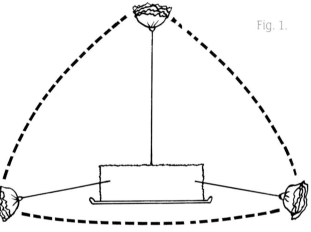

Fig. 1.

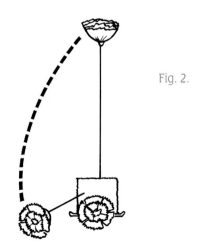

Fig. 2.

The material you will need
24 Apricot carnations
24 Pink roses
 2 Bunches baby's breath *(Gypsophila)*

DELPHINIUM PEDESTAL

The tall elegant beauty of delphiniums and golden rod make a natural basis for a huge pedestal arrangement. Without the column this design would look good in a fireplace.

How it is made

Prepare the bowl as shown on page 15 with two blocks of Oasis. Stable mechanics are vital.

Start with the beech leaves to provide a solid basis (Fig. 1). Then position seven delphiniums to set the shape; one large Cambridge blue colour as the top point and then three white at the sides and three purple delphiniums as the base line (Fig. 2). The top material should slope backwards slightly to help prevent the whole arrangement from toppling forward.

Go around the edge with 15 golden rod, as shown in Figure 3. Once again slope the top flowers slightly backwards.

Complete the base line with three Bells of Ireland, and two sprays of September flower. Now fill in the centre with delphiniums of various colours and golden rod. Use the remaining September flowers and white sprays of matricaria to provide a balance of brightness against any dark foliage.

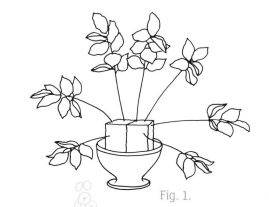

Fig. 1.

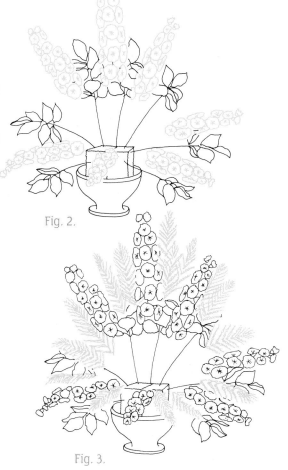

Fig. 2.

Fig. 3.

The material you will need

- 5 Cambridge blue delphinium
- 4 Dark blue delphinium
- 4 Purple delphinium
- 5 White delphinium
- 19 Stems golden rod (Solidago)
- 3 Bells of Ireland (Molucella)
- 13 Sprays September flowers (Aster)
- 3 Stems larkspur
- 5 Sprays white matricaria
- 5 Stems green spurge (Euphorbia)
- 7 Stems beech leaves

CANDLESTICK CURVES

The curving S-shape of this arrangement is ideal for an attractive candlestick. The light feathery ends to the shape contrast well with the repeated red and pink rhythm of carnations and tulips.

How it is made

Fix a foam anchor into the base of a candle cup using Oasis Fix. Push on a round of wet foam, previously thoroughly soaked in water. The foam should be at least 2 inches above the rim of the candle cup. Use Oasis Fix to fit the candle cup into the candlestick.

Several curving stems of broom are used to make the first strokes of the S-shape. The top piece is positioned slightly to the back of the foam while the lower piece is in front of the candlestick. A few stems of broom are cut short and used on the back right-hand edge and front left-hand edge (Fig. 1).

Amplify the basic shape with six carnations flowing in a rhythmical line from top left to bottom right. A similar, but longer line of tulips to the right of the carnations is positioned next (Fig. 2).

Now use the veronica foliage together with a few short stems of broom to cover the mechanics and to add bulk to the central focal point.

Position four tulips to the left of the carnation line. Avoid going outside the parameters of the broom. Now use a carnation on the left and on the right to balance and hold the design together (Fig. 3).

Use small pieces of foliage at the back to hide the foam and the stems.

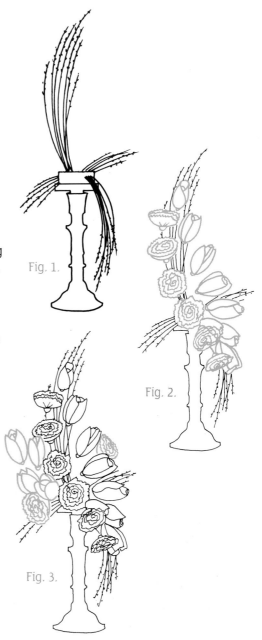

Fig. 1.

Fig. 2.

Fig. 3.

The material you will need
12 Tulips
 8 Carnations
36 Stems of broom (Cytisus)
12 Stems of variegated veronica (Hebe)

AUTUMN RICHNESS

This informal basket of rustic flowers relies on a strong shape and a blend of complementary colours to create an overall design. The points of the off-centred triangle shape are made strongly with evergreen foliage.

How it is made

Find a waterproof tray which will fit inside the basket and fix two foam anchors to the base of the tray. Push a block of green foam which has been previously soaked in water onto these anchors. Place this prepared tray inside the basket and tape into position (Fig. 1).

Start with the triangular outline using the rich leaves of butcher's broom or other evergreen foliage (Fig. 2).

Take three sprays of white chrysanthemums and three lily stems to amplify the triangular shape (Fig. 3).

Work around the edges of the arrangement with Peruvian lilies ensuring there is a balance between a point at the top and a similar point along the base.

Gradually fill in the centre of the design contrasting orange lilies with cream chrysanthemums. The solid colour of the pale chrysanthemums are used to make a focal point near to the base of the arrangement.

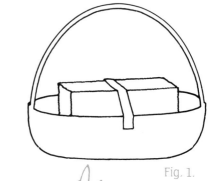

Fig. 1.

Fig. 2.

The material you will need

3 Sprays of white chrysanthemum
9 Stems of orange lilies
6 Stems of cream chrysanthemum
6 Stems Peruvian lily *(Alstroemeria)*
12 Stems butcher's broom *(Ruscus)*

Fig. 3.

PINK CIRCLE

A wide diversity of material is used to create this simple-looking all-round arrangement designed for a low coffee table. The regular frill of fern leaves gives it the look of a Victorian posy.

How it is made

Use a circular saucer to hold a round piece of wet foam, previously soaked.

Start around the edge with alternating leaves of leather leaf fern and Boston fern. They should form an outer fringe (Fig. 1). Use some of the lemon and pink carnations just above these leaves to form the first circle of colour.

Now define the height of the arrangement with one or two flowers in the centre (Fig. 2). Recess some of the variegated foliage, the spiky foliage and yellow chrysanthemums below this level of the final outline as shown in Figure 3.

Work up to the top now, mixing carnations and tulips as you go. These flowers will follow the outline with tulips being slightly more prominent than the other flowers. Remember to turn the arrangement around so that the dome shape is retained from all viewpoints. A turntable is an invaluable help.

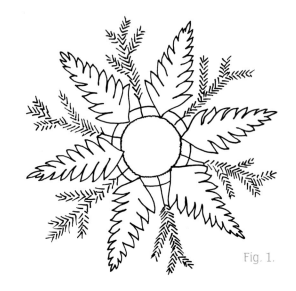

Fig. 1.

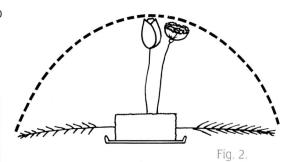

Fig. 2.

The material you will need
12 Pink tulips
12 Sprays of pink carnations
12 Sprays lemon carnations
 4 Sprays chrysanthemum
 6 Stems variegated veronica *(Hebe)*
 4 Leaves leather leaf fern (bracken)
 4 Leaves Boston fern *(Nephrolepis)*
 8 Pieces spiky foliage

Fig. 3.

ORANGE FIREPLACE

The grouping of similar material within an arrangement will create bold splashes of colour. The line and form, however, needs careful study to succeed. Here the sharp lines of orange gladioli contrast well with the bright spidery chrysanthemums and the informal lightness of dill.

How it is made
Fix two anchors to the flat base of the black bowl using Oasis Fix or other florist's clay. Thoroughly soak a block of green foam and push firmly onto these anchors.

Start with the two tallest stems of gladioli on the left-hand side, followed by two shorter stems on the right at the back (Fig. 1). Amplify these lines with more gladioli. On the left-hand side, the column of orange should reach right down to the bottom of the design (Fig. 2).

Fill in the centre with clusters of dill. Now create a sweeping spiral of yellow chrysanthemums starting just behind one of the gladiolus on the left and ending with a single flower prominently in the front (Fig. 3).

Use the grey conifer foliage around the bowl to hide unsightly stems and any mechanics.

The material you will need
14 Orange gladioli
 4 Sprays spiky yellow
    chrysanthemums
 8 Bunches dill
 8 Branches of conifer foliage

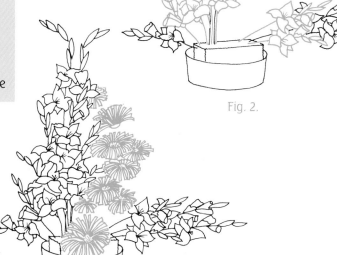

Fig. 1.

Fig. 2.

Fig. 3.

PINK PEDESTAL

When the occasion is grand enough and you have plenty of tall flowers at your disposal then this spectacular pedestal arrangement is within the capabilities of any arranger. To copy this design, check flower colours carefully for they should all blend together.

How it is made

Fix four anchors into the base of the pedestal container with florist's clay. Push one complete block of wet foam, previously soaked, at the back of the tray. Cut another slightly shorter and position this at the front. Tape blocks together and fix to tray with the same material (Fig. 1). An overall covering of chicken wire is also advisable.

Judge the size and scale of the arrangement carefully with the use of the first eight gladioli around the edge (Fig. 2). These will provide the radiating spokes which should be followed throughout. The top material should be sloping backwards to balance the necessary amount of stems which will eventually come forwards. Remember this is a physical balancing act as well as a blend of colours and shapes. Some woody material in the back will not only hide the foam but will help prevent the pedestal from falling over.

Next place ten alstroemeria around the edge between the gladioli (Fig. 3). Now work towards the centre using a mixture of flowering material and grey leaved eucalyptus. Try to give a change of texture between each flower.

Note that a bright focal point has been created using the contrast between two light pink gladioli and the richer spray of chrysanthemum.

The material you will need
16 Pink gladioli
16 Alstroemeria
 9 Sprays of dark pink chrysanthemum
19 White daisy flowers
13 Stems grey eucalyptus
 3 Stems trailing ivy

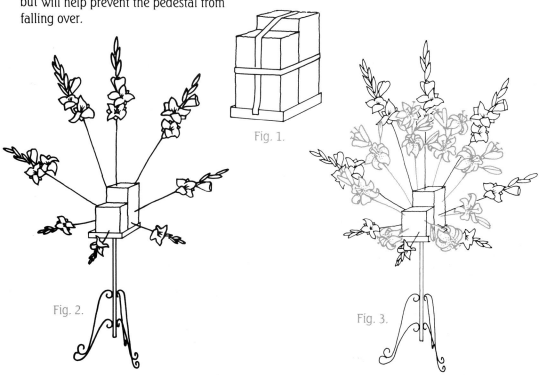

Fig. 1.

Fig. 2.

Fig. 3.

RED TABLE CENTRE

This long, low arrangement is ideal for the centre of a table, whether empty as pictured here, or dressed with silver and crystal for that elegant dinner party.

How it is made

Take an oblong tray and fit an anchor into the base. Push a block of florist foam previously soaked in water onto the anchor.

Start by going around the edge with eight roses to make an oval shape. Position a carnation between each rose seeing that the flowers are at slightly different levels above the table (Fig. 1). Go around this first layer with small bunches of baby's breath, making sure the stems are pushed into the foam.

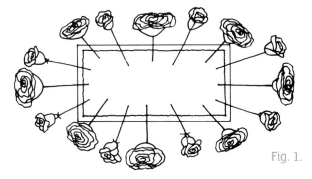

Fig. 1.

Set the maximum height at the centre with a rose (Fig. 2). Now create the cushion shape by gradually filling in from the base with a mixture of carnations and roses. The rose foliage should provide adequate cover of the foam, but if necessary use extra leaves to cover the mechanics.

As you work upwards fill in between the flowers with the baby's breath. Because the stems of this flower are fine it is difficult to fill in after the placement of the main flowers.

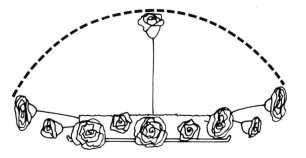

Fig. 2.

If you find this method of placing the baby's breath difficult, then you could start by covering the whole block with these sprays before you place any of the second layer of flowers.

The material you will need
18 Red carnations
24 Red roses
 4 Bunches baby's breath *(Gypsophila)*

CLASSIC LUXURY

This large display in a white urn owes its luxury touch to the lilies and to the contrasting textures of feathery astilbe and tight round heads of decorative allium.

How it is made

The urn will need to take two blocks of Oasis. Fix four anchors to the base of the urn with Oasis Fix. Take one block of wet foam, previously soaked and place this upright at the back. Cut another block just a little shorter and place at the front. Tape over the blocks to the urn and then cover with chicken wire, fixing around the edge with wire.

Fig. 1.

Start with the two stems of beech leaves to provide a strong base below the level of the urn's bowl. Now use pink and purple plumes of feathery astilbe to mark out the circular shape. See that the stems radiate from a central point (Fig. 2).

Use the small white sprays of matricaria around the circle (Fig. 3).

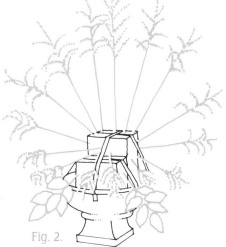

Fig. 2.

Fill the centre with a mixture of lilies and the scented heads of white bouvardia, giving each space but ensuring the lilies are the central point of interest.

To complete the arrangement use the drumstick heads of decorative allium in a crescent as shown. Their strong shape and colour is useful around the edge and to provide points of interest in the centre. To finish, use a few heads of pink astilbe in among the lilies.

The material you will need
10 Stargazer lilies
10 Decorative allium (Allium sphaerocephalon)
20 Salmon pink astilbe
12 Purple astilbe
10 Sprays matricaria
 8 White bouvardia

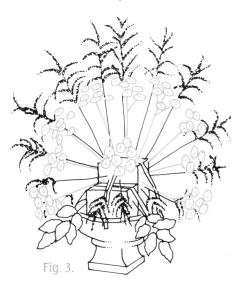

Fig. 3.

OVAL ON OAK

The rich colours of this all-round arrangement are needed to blend in with the solid oak table. The mixture of bright red, yellow and mauve illustrates that in nature it is difficult to mix colours that really clash.

How it is made

The low tray which forms the base of this arrangement is insignificant. See that it is waterproof and will not scratch the table. Fix two foam anchors to the base using florist's clay. Trim a block of Oasis foam, previously soaked in water, to fit and push onto the anchors.

Take small pieces of September flowers to make the base line (Fig. 1). Cover the outside of foam with variegated foliage and a few scabious. This will provide the recessed detail.

Use a rose bud in the centre to set the maximum height of the arrangement (Fig. 2).

Start filling in the dome shape from the base upwards. Fix material as you go, allowing space for each flower to dominate in different places.

To finish, use some pieces of September flowers to break the smooth level of the dome, especially around the top. This change of depth from recessed, semi-hidden material to the main structure and then to feathery flowers outside the outline helps to create visual interest.

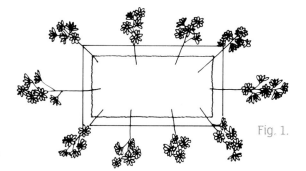

Fig. 1.

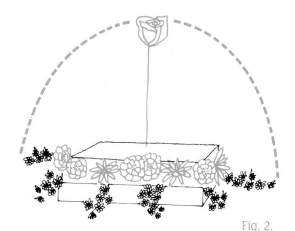

Fig. 2.

The material you will need
20 Scabious
16 Roses
20 Sprays September flowers
20 Cream chrysanthemum with
   yellow centre
 8 Pieces variegated daphne foliage

CREAMY ROSES

This long lasting combination of lilies and roses shows how a monochromatic colour theme can still have textural interest. This is achieved with a contrast in flower size and the use of sharp edged ferns.

How it is made

Use two foam anchors and fit to the base of the attractive low bowl with Oasis Fix or other florists clay. Push a block of wet foam onto the anchors.

Start by creating the triangular outline of the design with the fern leaves (Fig. 1).

Now place the top-most spray of lilies within the confines of the triangular shape. Place two more lily stems down through the centre, ensuring that there is an open flower near the centre of the triangle and at the base. The remaining two stems use buds on either side of this line to keep the triangular design (Fig. 2).

Now start to fill in the shape with the cream roses. Define the outer points of the triangle and the base line with roses and then gradually work up. Don't strip all the foliage from the rose stems as these leaves will help to hide the foam.

Fill with a few fern leaves dotted around the centre of the arrangement.

The material you will need
  5 Sprays of lilies in cream and peach
18 Cream roses
25 Sword fern *(Nephrolepis)*

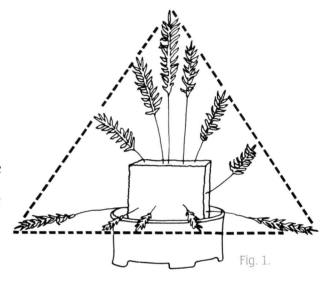

Fig. 1.

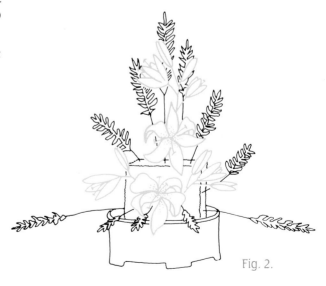

Fig. 2.

A F R I C A N S I M P L I C I T Y

The bold simplicity of five heads of African lily in a matt black vase is stunning. You will need to position the arrangement against a simple background or the carefully created line and flow of stems will be lost.

How it is made

The precise placement of the stems is vital to this arrangement. While you could try to use chicken wire to fill the vase and hold the stems in place the most satisfactory way is to use a block of green Oasis.

Fix a foam anchor into the bottom of the vase with florist's clay. Trim the block after it has been thoroughly soaked into shape so that it can be pushed into the neck with a tight fit (Fig. 1). Trim off excess foam so that only ½ inch (1 cm) of Oasis is showing.

The tallest African lily is placed in position first. This should be at the back of the foam and central to the vase. Carefully measure the next two flowers which are to go on the right-hand side and position them slightly lower and gently sloping away from the vertical. The principle that all the stems should look as if they are coming from a central point is amply illustrated with this design (Fig. 2).

Now position the two remaining African lilies on the left-hand side of the vertical. They should fit between the heads already in position.

Finish off with the leaves of the plantain lily. Two leaves are used in the centre to hide the flower stems and four around the vase to hide the mechanics. The last leaf is the variegated one which is stitched back at the point to give a curved effect. Placing this leaf at the front gives a visual link in line and shape between the container and the arrangement.

Fig. 1.

Fig. 2.

The material you will need
    5 Heads of African lily *(Agapanthus)*
    8 Plantain lily leaves *(Hosta)*

SILVER BASKET

This informal country look has been achieved with a variety of old-fashioned flowers. The different types of silver foliage help to hold the design together.

How it is made
Take a round piece of foam, previously soaked in water, and put it in a waterproof polythene bag. Place a solid object into the bottom of the basket to get the height of the foam correct. When the bag is placed into the basket and the top opened there should be 1 inch of foam showing (Fig. 1).

Fig. 1.

Start with the two central spires of pink larkspur to define the maximum height. Now cover the foam with silver leaves of the cineraria (Fig. 2).

Use the remaining stems of silver foliage to provide interesting spikes and fill in with the larkspur flowers. One or two larkspur stems should overhang the rim of the basket.

Now use the red-centred pink 'Doris' to provide the central core of colour. Once again use some of the stems below the level of the basket rim to provide a link between the flowers and the container.

The material you will need
9 Pink and white larkspur
3 Stems silver foliage *(Pyrus salicifolia)*
5 Bunches cineraria 'Silver Dust'
12 Pinks *(Dianthus 'Doris')*

Fig. 2.

FREESIAS & CANDLES

Simple, stylish and full of fragrance. Multi-coloured freesias are mixed with some light foliage to make an arrangement instead of a vase of flowers with straight stems. The candles could be omitted if the double brass candle holder which fits over the rim of the vase is unavailable.

How it is made

Cut a piece of soaked Oasis into roughly the size and shape of the vase and wedge into the top.

Start by placing the trailing ivy and fern around the edge. They should overhang the edge but not quite reach the base of the vase (Fig. 1). Fill in around the edge of the foam with Mexican orange and some more fern. This should hide the foam in the vase.

Fig. 1.

Define the height of the arrangement with two stems of freesias in the centre. These should be about one and a half times the height of the vase (Fig. 2).

Remember that this is an all round dome shape so the side views are just as important as the shape from head on. Work down the height, mixing different coloured freesia stems and ensuring the buds point in different directions. Keep turning the arrangement around so that you work from different angles.

At various points include Mexican orange and fern foliage recessed deep into the dome shape. This will cover the forest of straight flowers stems which would otherwise be on view.

The material you will need
36 Freesias
 6 Mexican orange stems
10 Pieces fern
10 Ivy stems

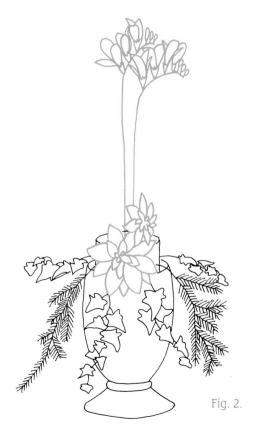

Fig. 2.

INFORMAL BEAUTY

Displaying fresh flowers in natural sunlight is a delight, even in this unusual setting on the floor. Here an informal bowl of lilies and chrysanthemums adds a country look to this conservatory.

How it is made

Take two blocks of Oasis and wedge into the top of the vase. See that an inch or two of foam is visible over the lip of the vase. Cover with chicken wire (Fig. 1).

Start the arrangement with the tallest lily stem in the centre. Surround this with asparagus fern and use more of this foliage around the edge of the vase. Now evenly space three sprays of chrysanthemums just below the central lily stem (Fig. 2).

Fill in the dome shape with sprays of chrysanthemum, ensuring some of the flowers overlap the edge of the vase.

Now on slightly longer stems arrange the lilies around the vase so that they dominate the arrangement.

Fill in with any remaining asparagus fern to contrast the bold lily flowers with the feathery lightness of this greenery.

The material you will need
10 Pink lilies
10 Sprays of pink chrysanthemums
10 Stems of asparagus fern

Fig. 1.

Fig. 2.

SCENT OF SWEET PEAS

Here are enough sweet peas to scent a ballroom. The luxury of being able to use these many flowers is amply rewarded by a multi-coloured arrangement which will last a long time.

How it is made

Prepare a tray or container with two anchors firmly stuck to the base with Oasis Fix. Push two blocks of wet foam previously soaked for a couple of hours onto the anchors. Tape the block to the tray. Position the tray inside the basket and tape down to secure (Fig. 1).

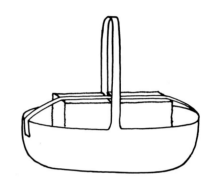

Fig. 1.

There will be no foliage on the sweet pea stems so it is important to cover the foam with asparagus fern before you position one flower. To add some bulk we have also used some fern at the back and overhanging the sides (Fig. 2).

All sweet pea stems should look as if they radiate from a central point. Start with an edging of light salmon to set the parameters in which you are working (Fig. 3).

Fill in with the sweet peas, mixing colours as you progress. Some short stemmed flowers should be used within the arrangement to add depth.

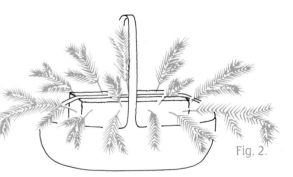

Fig. 2.

Save the darkest colours to provide a central point of interest around the basket handle and to add depth to the outer edges.

The material you will need

2 Bunches asparagus fern
9 Bunches of sweet peas (10 per bunch)

Select the colours of the sweet peas with care. We used about six different colours in the pastel pink, salmon, and soft mauve end of the colour wheel.

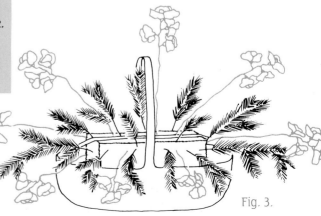

Fig. 3.

CELEBRATION CENTRE

Here a sophisticated table centre which has ingredients taken directly from the wild. Oak leaves, blackberry fruits and yarrow bring the scents and sights of the countryside alongside roses and carnations.

How it is made

Use a waterproof saucer and fit a foam anchor to the base with Oasis Fix. Push on a round of wet foam previously soaked in water for several hours.

Start by going around the base of the arrangement with a mixture of blackberry sprays, viburnum and eucalyptus foliage (Fig. 1). One stem of blackberries is placed centrally to determine the overall height (Fig. 2). Then use the remaining blackberry heads to outline the dome shape which you are creating.

Fig. 1.

Fill in the shape with pink carnations, alstroemeria and the foliage. Some of this material should be on shorter stems so that the flower heads are recessed below the eventual level of the roses.

Now position the roses around the arrangement mixing buds beside more open blooms wherever possible.

Finally use the white September flowers to provide delicate points of interest above the level of the roses.

Fig. 2.

The material you will need
30 Roses
10 Sprays of pink carnations
 6 Stems alstroemeria
10 Sprays September flowers
12 Heads blackberry fruits
   Ivy foliage
   Eucalyptus foliage
   Viburnum foliage

GOLDEN GLORY

Careful choice of colours gives a fresh clean look to this mono-chromatic arrangement. Note the mixture of textures and the use of just a few spiky gladioli-like flowers to break the outline.

How it is made

The low white bowl needs four foam anchors fixed into its base with florist's clay. Push two Oasis blocks, previously well soaked, onto the anchors.

Start by using two stocks at the back and centrally to define the height of the arrangement. Then use stocks along the edges and along the base line to set the triangular shape (Fig. 1). Use stems of the green spurge foliage around the edges to give a feathery outline.

Use the strong colour of the Peruvian lilies all around the main body of the design. When next to white or cream they will provide the necessary contrast (Fig. 2). Now use the four sprays of cream chrysanthemums and the remaining stocks to complete the central area.

Complete the arrangement with a few pieces of spurge foliage followed by the spiky contrast of the smallish white gladioli-like flowers of acidanthera.

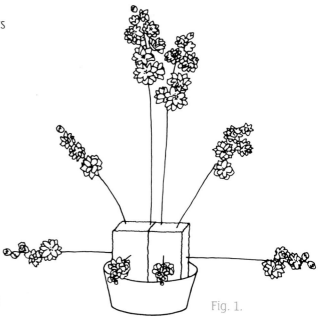

Fig. 1.

The material you will need
10 White stocks
15 Stems green spurge *(Euphorbia robiae)*
10 Peruvian lilies *(Alstroemeria)*
 4 Sprays cream chrysanthemum
10 White acidanthera *(Gladiolus callianthus)*

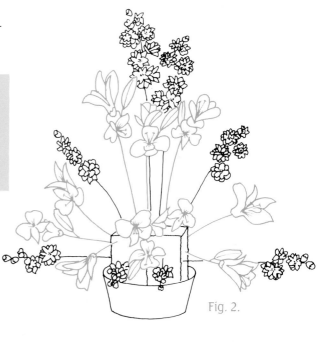

Fig. 2.

FIGURINE & FREESIAS

The traditional soap stone base needs a formal outline and this inverted crescent works well in a guest room. The scent of the freesias will add to the memory of an attractive arrangement.

How it is made

Put some Oasis Fix onto the base of a foam anchor and fit to the bowl of the soap stone base. Push on a round of wet foam firmly onto the anchor.

Start by defining the height of the arrangement with the central piece of golden rod. Position at the back of the foam. Now create the base line with three freesias and three pieces of grey leaved trailing stems. They should all be below the rim of the base and frame the figurine (Fig. 1).

Fill in the outline with four freesias and two heads of golden rod (Fig. 2).

Before you start to complete the arrangement use some small pieces of golden rod and grey-leaved cytisus to cover the surface of the green foam.

Now use love-in-a-mist heads and the lemon chrysanthemum sprays to fill in the circle. The largest lemon spray should be placed in the middle to form the focal point.

Finish by placing the remaining eight freesias strategically in the centre. Use any remaining material to cover the stems and tidy up the back of the arrangement.

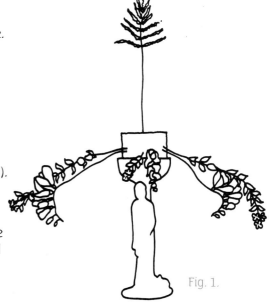

Fig. 1.

The material you will need

14 Mauve freesias
 7 Golden rod (Solidago)
11 Love-in-a-mist seed pods (Nigella)
 5 Stems grey-leaved cytisus
 8 Pale lemon spray chrysanthemums

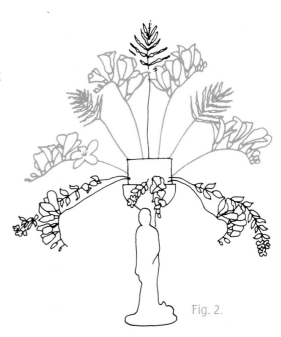

Fig. 2.

UPRIGHT GERBERAS

The flowers and foliage are so striking that they need to be used with some restraint. This strong vertical design works well on a desk where space is at a premium.

How it is made

Prepare a circular container with a foam anchor fixed to the base with Oasis Fix. Push on a round of wet foam previously soaked in water.

The size and placement of the cycas leaves is important to success. Start with the tallest and then arrange the other four as shown in Figure 1. Note that the front right leaf has been trimmed with scissors to keep within a small base-line.

Insert a wire up the stem of each gerbera to maintain rigidity. Cut to length and arrange as shown in Figure 2. Note that while there is a common line to follow, the flowers all point in different directions and one is recessed closely by the base of the cycas leaves to give depth.

Some upright bear grass stems have been used to amplify the vertical line and to link the foliage with the flowers.

Fill in the right-hand side with roses, ensuring some appear between the gerberas to avoid a green dividing space between the two types of blooms. See that some roses are recessed at the base to hide the mechanics.

The material you will need
  5 Pink gerberas
  6 Cycas leaves
14 Pink roses
10 Stems bear grass

Fig. 1.

Fig. 2.

BRIDAL PEDESTAL

Overall shape and colour co-ordination are important in this marquee setting as the arrangement will be viewed by most guests from quite a distance. The choice of material in blending pink and white co-ordinates well with the interior.

How it is made

Follow the directions on page 15 for underlying mechanics of foam and tape to create a stable base.

Start by defining the outline of the shape using ten branches of beech leaves. The top branches should lean backwards (Fig. 1). The red-berried foliage should be positioned next followed by white gladioli stems between the beech leaves (Fig. 2).

Go around the edge with Peruvian lilies and white September flowers.

Now position the lilies. Choose two stems to form the focal point in the centre and three other stems radiating above. Use the white spray chrysanthemums to add contrast to the centre, making sure the largest head is used near the focal point.

The pink carnations are mainly positioned in the centre, providing a concentrated colour intensity.

Finally finish off with the spiky stems of white gladioli all radiated from the central focal point.

The material you will need
10 Sprays white September flowers
5 Sprays Stargazer lilies
5 Sprays white chrysanthemum
10 Sprays Peruvian lily *(Alstroemeria)*
14 White gladiolus
12 Pink carnations
Beech foliage
Red-berried rowan *(Sorbus)*

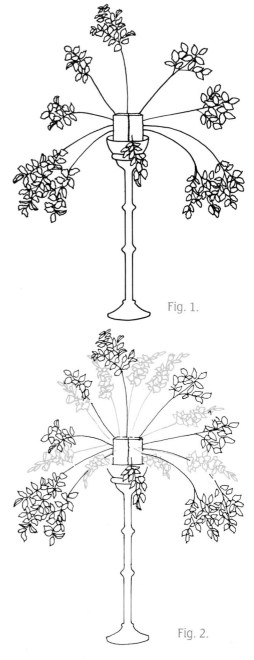

Fig. 1.

Fig. 2.

WELCOME WREATH

More like a star burst than a circular wreath, this traditional front door decoration is jammed with different material and topped by a professional bow.

How it is made

Buy a plastic circular wreath base which is already fitted with Oasis foam. Soak well in water and position flat on a table. If there is no hook then use strong wire to create the necessary hanging position before you add any material.

Start by using pieces of spruce foliage to create the radiating outline (Fig. 1). See that this foliage reaches the level of the table.

Fig. 1.

Now use the variegated holly and blue spruce and pine foliage to cover the ring. Make sure there is enough variegated holly foliage to feature all round the circle for this adds lightness to the wreath.

Add a wire stem to each fir cone (Fig. 2) and twist three stems together to make a bunch. Include these at different angles.

Fill in the centre with foliage as necessary. Finally push the red berries into position and top off with the red bow.

Fig. 2.

The material you will need
Spruce foliage
Variegated holly foliage
Blue spruce foliage
Pine foliage
Larch cones
Spruce cones
Ribbon bow

CHRISTMAS CARNATIONS

The classic L-shape arrangement is ideal for a mantlepiece display. Variegated holly and red candles ensure a traditional feel and unusual lotus seed heads add a different texture.

How it is made

Use a narrow waterproof tray which will sit safely on the mantlepiece. Fix two foam anchors to the base and push on a block of Oasis foam, previously soaked in water.

Start the L-shape outline with the painted stems of birch twigs (Fig. 1).

The candles are cut to different lengths and pushed directly into the wet foam. Use the holly as the major points of the triangle (Fig. 2) and the rest of the different foliage to cover the foam block and create the immediate shape.

Position the lotus seed heads deep within the foliage to add weight to the base line.

Now use the carnations to fill out the shape pointing them all in slightly different directions.

Finish off with a few strategically placed twigs of beech to ensure their red points are evenly situated around the triangular outline.

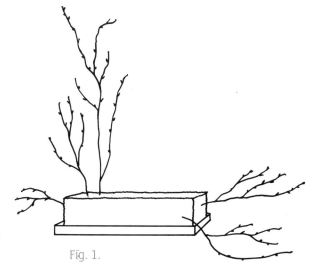

Fig. 1.

The material you will need
12 Red carnations
 3 Lotus seed heads
 7 Stems variegated holly foliage
 9 Stems Leyland foliage *(Cupressocyparis Leylandii)*
11 Pieces of Spruce foliage *(Picea)*
 8 Beech twigs painted red
 2 Candles

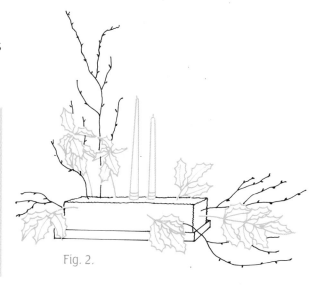

Fig. 2.

CONES & CANDLES

The contrast of a group of pure white candles against the dark textured beauty of three types of cones and three different sorts of evergreen foliage provides an impressive combination.

How it is made

For a long-lasting arrangement use green wet foam as the base to hold the fresh material. The evergreen foliage may not take up a lot of water but it allows you the option of misting regularly over the leaves with plain water.

Fix two foam anchors into the bottom of the bowl and push on a block of foam previously soaked in water.

Start by defining the height with a piece of branching yew and then the two base points of the triangle with blue cedar branches (Fig. 1).

The five white pencil candles are pushed directly into the Oasis at different depths to create a gentle spiral shape.

Use some evergreen foliage around the edge of the bowl to hide the mechanics and soften the hard edge. Wire each of the cones separately and use as shown in Figure 2.

The artichoke heads usually have a stem but if this is not long enough add a double leg wire so that they can be placed in position on the right-hand side.

Finish off with foliage to fill in the outline and hide the stems of material and the base of the candles.

Fig. 1.

Fig. 2.

The material you will need
2 Artichoke heads
1 Piece of yew foliage *(Taxus)*
5 Pieces of blue cedar *(Cedrus atlantica glauca)*
5 Pieces pine foliage *(Pinus mugo)*
3 Cones of blue cedar
5 Ribbon cones
2 Pine cones
5 Thin candles

GOLDEN CIRCLET

A wall decoration which uses the gilded circles of intertwined vine stems is ideal at Christmas time. The fresh foliage should enhance the base and not overwhelm the golden ring.

How it is made

Take a small piece of Oasis foam about three inches long, one inch wide and one inch deep. Soak well in water. Now use florist tape to secure this in position at the base of the ring (Fig. 1).

Start with dark green foliage around the edge of the oval shape. Keep the outline in proportion to the size of the ring – just a little wider and not too deep. Overlap this original layer with contrasting green foliage.

Now take the blue spruce foliage and fill in the centre of the arrangement. Wire the fir cone and position as the focal point directly above the ring base.

The ribbon bow is made in three sections. First make several loops of ribbon and pinch the ends together. Use a stub wire to tightly bind the ribbon ends together and to make a stem. Push this upwards into the foam just below the fir cone. Now make two 'tails' of different length. Cut a 'V' shape from one end of a length of ribbon and then use wire to make a double leg wire stem around the opposite tapered end. Position the 'tails' separately.

Use the three lotus seed heads to finish off, two at the bottom right, just below the bow, and one at the top diagonally opposite.

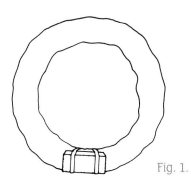

Fig. 1.

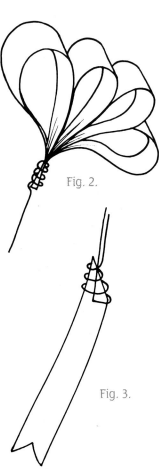

Fig. 2.

Fig. 3.

The material you will need
  Pine foliage *(Pinus)*
  Blue spruce foliage *(Picea)*
  Fir foliage *(Abies)*
3 Lotus seed heads
1 Fir cone
  Red ribbon

ROSE TABLE CENTRE

The ideal shape and colouring for a winter dinner party. The flowers are kept low enough to allow easy conversation and the white candles will add a sparkle to the silver and glasses.

How it is made

The base is a simple waterproof tray with low edges. Fix two foam anchors to the base with Oasis Fix. Push a block of Oasis previously soaked onto the anchors.

Start by going around the edges with the foliage making a long oval (Fig. 1). Now follow the same shape, alternating roses with carnations (Fig. 2).

Place the three candles into position in a straight line down the centre of the oval. Push the outside two just a little further down into the foam to give a variation of height.

Cover the foam with short pieces of holly and evergreen foliage. Make sure that the spaces between the candles are covered.

Now build up the flowering outline keeping carnation just slightly recessed below the level of the beautiful roses which should dominate.

Fig. 1.

Fig. 2.

The material you will need
24 Red roses
24 Yellow carnations
   Holly foliage
   Yew foliage
3 Candles

WHITE CHRISTMAS

Ideal for Christmas, Hogmanay or Burns Night this pure white arrangement relies on a strong colour for the ribbon bow and matching candles.

How it is made

Fix a foam anchor into the metal base with Oasis Fix. Push a round of wet foam onto the anchor after soaking in water for a couple of hours.

Cut one of the candles slightly shorter than the other and push them both directly into the wet foam. Ensure they are vertical and then place the ribbon bow centrally.

Use three pieces of ivy and three pieces of conifer foliage to make the trailing base points (Fig. 1). Then position pieces of blue conifer foliage to form the background and start the outline.

Six of the freesias are placed around the edges to define the crescent shape (Fig. 2).

Now fill in the centre with sprays of white chrysanthemums mixed with foliage and freesias. Try to position the freesias so that they face in different directions. This will show the overall form of this beautiful flower. Make sure that there is space around the candle to allow them to be burnt without danger.

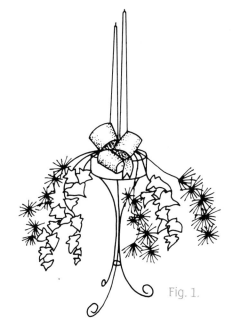

Fig. 1.

The material you will need

18 White freesias
 4 Sprays white chrysanthemums
 3 Stems trailing variegated ivy
 8 Pieces blue cedar foliage
 3 Long stems pine foliage
 2 Candles
 1 Bow

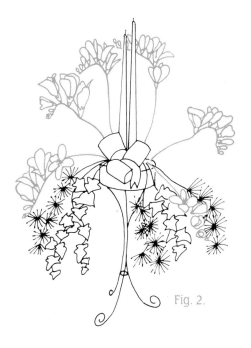

Fig. 2.

CHRISTMAS GARLAND

While the centre of attention is the beauty of the golden bows the real key to success with this arrangement is the lush use of foliage, using as many different varieties as you can obtain.

How it is made

Take a piece of rope and cut to the right length. Before adding foliage first tie wires to the three hanging points so that the correct curve is achieved.

In the photograph our central hanging point is a picture hook while the top points are screws which have been positioned through the coving.

Start the garland from one end, wiring different foliage along the length of the rope. Mix yew alongside variegated holly, spruce and cypress making sure that one piece overlaps the stem and wire from the previous pieces (Fig. 1). When you get to the end make a 'return' so that the last of the rope and the foliage stems are hidden (Fig. 2).

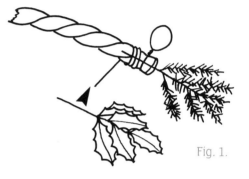

Fig. 1.

Once the foliage garland is complete hang from the wire rings in position on the wall and check the curves. Adjust as necessary. Wire the three golden bows into position. Page 16 shows how these can be made in advance.

Now wire the golden grapes and walnuts into position at suitable intervals. Three cinnamon sticks are tied together with red ribbon and then wired into position. Finish off with red berries and fir cones at regular intervals to add points of interest.

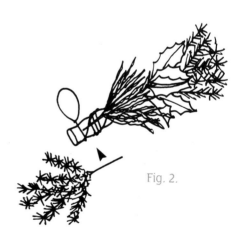

Fig. 2.

The material you will need
   Holly foliage and berries
   Yew foliage
   Cypress foliage
   Spruce foliage
6 Sticks cinnamon
6 Walnuts
6 Fir cones
3 Golden bows
2 Bunches golden grapes

TARTAN CIRCLE

Just seven white chrysanthemums hold this Yuletide arrangement together as an entity. Once again the variety of different foliage colours and textures is important to add variety.

How it is made

Buy a circular Oasis holder 12 inches in diameter. Thoroughly soak the foam in water before you start. Push the candles into the foam evenly around the circle, making sure they are vertical (Fig. 1).

Cut the evergreen foliage in short pieces and go around the edge of the circle mixing blue spruce with juniper and variegated holly (Fig. 2). Use pieces of hebe and other foliage to cover the surface of the foam, seeing that the inside is also covered.

Now place the seven white chrysanthemums around the circle. Ensure that they are pointing in different directions.

Wire loops of tartan ribbon as shown on page 86 and push into position at four points between each candle.

Finish off with the seed heads. Make four bunches of poppy heads by wiring three per bunch and place around the circle. Then wire two bunches of walnuts, three per bunch, before positioning towards the centre of the arrangement. Finally use the lotus heads and red holly berries to add extra colour.

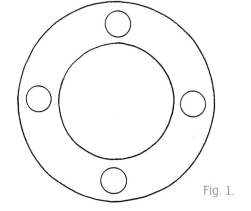

Fig. 1.

The material you will need
  7 White chrysanthemums
12 Poppy seed heads
  5 Lotus seed heads
  6 Walnuts
     Holly foliage
     Blue spruce foliage
     Juniper foliage
     Variegated hebe foliage
  4 Red candles

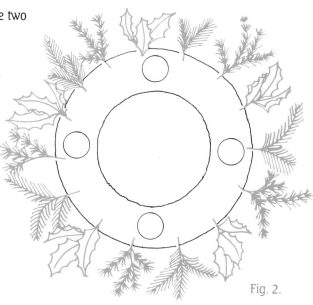

Fig. 2.

INDEX